I0821858

My Horse
Candice Letkeman
EYEDISCOVER

Go to www.eyediscover.com and enter this book's unique code.

BOOK CODE

B738734

EYEDISCOVER brings you optic readalongs that support active learning.

Published by AV² by Weigl
350 5th Avenue, 59th Floor New York, NY 10118
Website: www.eyediscover.com

Library of Congress Control Number: 2017930717

ISBN 978-1-4896-5665-0 (hardcover)

Printed in the United States of America
in Brainerd, Minnesota
1 2 3 4 5 6 7 8 9 0 21 20 19 18 17

082017
020317

Editor: Katie Gillespie
Designer: Mandy Christiansen

Weigl acknowledges Getty Images, iStock, and Shutterstock as the primary image suppliers for this title.

EYEDISCOVER provides enriched content, optimized for tablet use, that supplements and complements this book. EYEDISCOVER books strive to create inspired learning and engage young minds in a total learning experience.

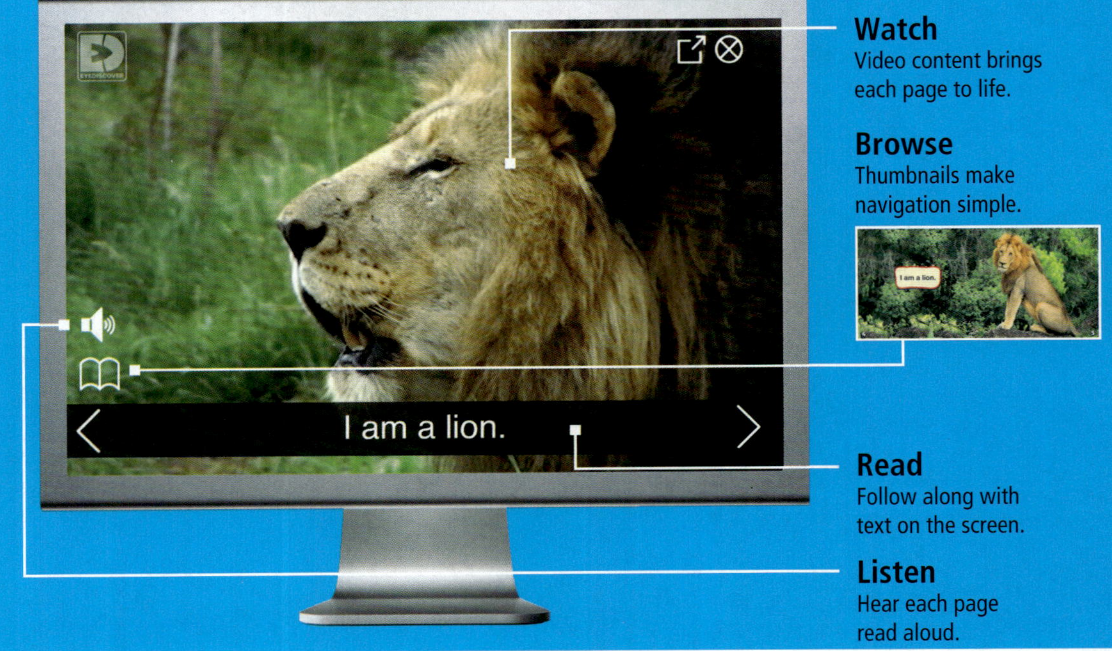

Watch
Video content brings each page to life.

Browse
Thumbnails make navigation simple.

Read
Follow along with text on the screen.

Listen
Hear each page read aloud.

Your EYEDISCOVER Optic Readalongs come alive with...

Audio
Listen to the entire book read aloud.

Video
High resolution videos turn each spread into an optic readalong.

OPTIMIZED FOR

TABLETS

WHITEBOARDS

COMPUTERS

AND MUCH MORE!

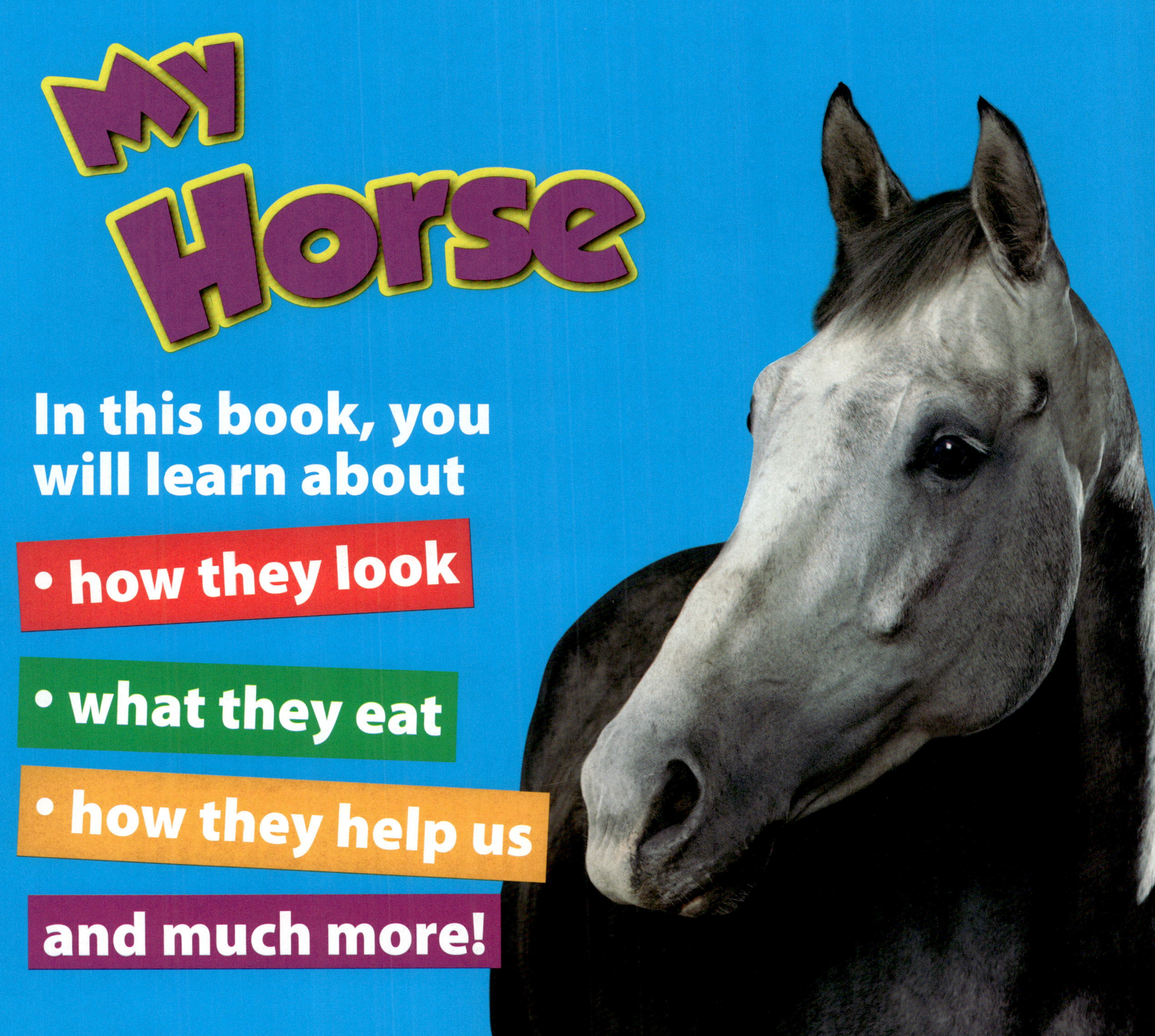
My Horse
In this book, you will learn about
• how they look
• what they eat
• how they help us
and much more!

There are more than 300 kinds of horses on Earth. They have many different colors and patterns.

Some horses are pets that people ride. Horses are loyal and remember people who have been kind to them.

TAGHeuer
POLICE

Other horses have jobs. Police horses control crowds or help find lost people.

Horses have long legs and can run very fast. Some horses run in races and win trophies.

Horses are smart. They can learn to do tricks such as taking a bow.

Horses have very large eyes. They can see in almost every direction.

Horses graze on grass and eat hay. They also like treats such as carrots, sugar cubes, and bread.

Horses have long manes and tails that must be brushed often. Some horses get fancy hairstyles.

Horses are gentle when they feel safe. They can help people who are sad or worried feel better.

HORSES BY THE NUMBERS

Foals can stand on their own a **few hours** after birth.

Horses can **live** to be **35** years old.

The **height** of a horse is measured in **hands**. One hand is equal to **4 inches**. (10 centimeters)

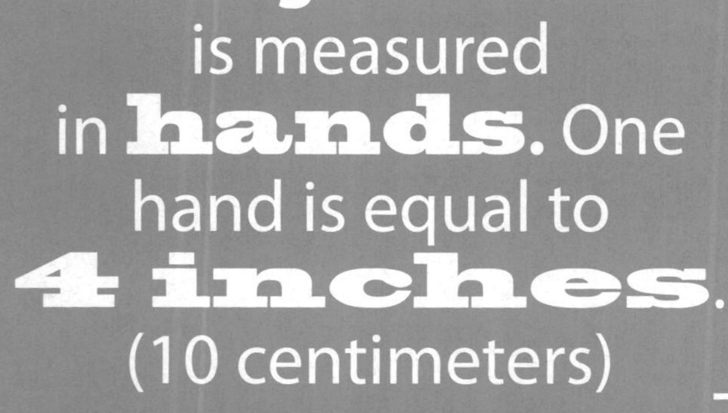

When a horse gallops, **all four feet** leave the ground.

There are about **60 million** horses on Earth.

A horse can **drink** as much as **10 gallons** of water in **one day**. (38 liters)

KEY WORDS

Research has shown that as much as 65 percent of all written material published in English is made up of 300 words. These 300 words cannot be taught using pictures or learned by sounding them out. They must be recognized by sight. This book contains 47 common sight words to help young readers improve their reading fluency and comprehension. This book also teaches young readers several important content words, such as proper nouns. These words are paired with pictures to aid in learning and improve understanding.

Page	Sight Words First Appearance
4	and, are, different, Earth, have, kinds, many, more, of, on, than, there, they
6	been, people, some, that, them, to, who
9	find, help, or, other
10	can, in, long, run, very
12	a, as, do, learn, such
15	almost, every, eyes, large, see
17	also, eat, like
19	be, get, must, often
21	when

Page	Content Words First Appearance
4	colors, horses, patterns
6	pets
9	crowds, jobs, police horses
10	legs, races, trophies
12	bow, tricks
15	direction
17	bread, carrots, grass, hay, sugar cubes, treats
19	hairstyles, manes, tails

Watch
Video content brings each page to life.

Browse
Thumbnails make navigation simple.

Read
Follow along with text on the screen.

Listen
Hear each page read aloud.

Go to www.eyediscover.com and enter this book's unique code.

BOOK CODE

B738734